The

BIT CHING

Book of Change

In the left column, choose the outer force that most closely describes the challenge at hand. Then, in the top row, find the word that best describes your unsettled feeling (inner force). The number at the intersection indicates the chapter to seek for counsel.

Or just pick up the book and read it.

OUTER FORCE ▼ (The challenge you face)	▼ INNER FORCE (What you feel about the challenge)							
	OVERLOAD	APPREHENSION	FRUSTRATION	ANGER/GREED	CONFUSION	DISTRACTION	EGO	RESIGNATION
OBSTACLE	1	2	3	13	6	4	7	8
CROSSROADS	11	40	42	16	12	10	15	14
PRESSURE	19	21	18	41	22	20	23	17
BULLSHIT	5	26	32	27	29	28	30	25
MORONS	39	36	34	35	37	33	55	38
INTERACTION	47	45	46	48	9	31	24	44
NEED TO LEAD	51	56	54	43	52	50	49	53
SUCCESS	57	59	61	60	62	58	63	64

The
BIT CHING
Book of Change

Reinterpreting the Ancient Wisdom of The *I Ching* to
Deal with Modern Day Morons & Confusion

By James Gentile and Russell Slocum

[handwritten: Melanie — Best of luck, hope this occasionally helps, Russ]

[handwritten: Be Profound, Be Funny or Be Quiet Woxxxxx 2012]

PERIPATE PRESS
Wyomissing, Pennsylvania

The Bit Ching Book of Change: Reinterpreting the Ancient Wisdom of
The I Ching to Deal with Modern Day Morons & Confusion

Copyright © 2011 by James Gentile and Russell Slocum. Printed in U.S.A.

For information email peripatepress@theslocumgroup.com.

ISBN-10: 0615523498
ISBN-13: 978-0615523491
Library of Congress Control Number 2011937689

Acknowledgements

There is nothing scholarly about this book. It is primarily Jim Gentile's cumulative interpretation and application of various translations of the *I Ching* as well as other books on Eastern Thought. While nothing has been consciously excerpted from any other source, countless other works have influenced Jim Gentile's life and philosophy, and thereby this book. Jim's personal favorites are the *I Ching or Book of Changes*, by Brian Browne Walker (St. Martin's Griffin); *Tao Te Ching*, by Stephen Mitchell (HarperPerennial); and *I Ching Wisdom*, Wu Wei (Power Press).

We would also like to acknowledge the insights and inspiration of Sun Tzu's *The Art of War*, separate editions translated by Thomas Cleary (Shambhala), and edited by James Clavell (Delta); *Sun Tzu For Execution*, Steven Michaelson (Adams Business);*Sun Tzu for Success*, Gerald Michaelson (Adams Media); *Way of the Peaceful Warrior*, *Wisdom of the Peaceful Warrior*, *No Ordinary Moments*, and *The Laws of Spirit*, all four books by Dan Millman, (H.J. Kramer); *Everyday Enlightenment*, Dan Millman (Warner Books); *Living on Purpose*, Dan Millman (new World Library); *The Sacred Path of the Warrior*, Chogyam Trungpa (Shambhala), *Instant Zen*, translated by Thomas Cleary (North Atlantic); *The Insights for a New Way of Living* series by Osho (St. Martin Griffin); Thich Nhat Hanh's *Peace is Every Step* (Bantam), *Touching Peace* (Parallax Press) and *Being Peace* (Parallax Press); *Quiet Mind, Fearless Heart* by Brian Luke Seaward (Wiley) ; *Quiet Your Mind* by John Selby (Inner Ocean); *Zen Lessons: The Art of Leadership*, and *Instant Zen: Waking Up in the Present*, both translated by Thomas Cleary and published by North Atlantic Books; three books by Don Miguel Ruiz and published by Amber-Allen: *The Voice of Knowledge*, *The Mastery of Love*, and *The Four Agreements Companion Book*; *The Wisdom of the native Americans*, edited by Kent Nerburn (New World Library); *The Tao of Inner Peace*, Diane Dreher (Harper Perennial); *The Tao of Contemplation*, Jasmin Lee Cori (Samuel Weiser); *Keep Going: The Art of Perseverance*, Joseph Marshall III (Sterling), *The Book of Secrets*, Deepak Chopra (Harmony); *The Tao of Willie*, Willie Nelson with Turk Pipkin (Putnam); *The Second Book of Tao*, Stephen Mitchell (Penguin); *Thinking Body, Dancing Mind*, by Chunglian Al Huang and Jerry Lynch; and James Redfield's *The Celestine Prophecy*, *The Tenth Insight*, and *The Secret of Shambhala* (Warner Books).

Graphic Design
Our deepest thanks to graphic designers Mark Grounard, Keith Nicholas and Shawn Reed, who for many years have helped our ideas look extraordinarily good.

Cover design, turtle illustration, chart of inner/outer forces & Working Dog characters: Mark Grounard
Page format & typography: Keith Nicholas
Layout of the text & file prep: Shawn Reed
Individual chapter characters and translations: Dragon Artworks

To my wife Denise, my daughters Jessica & Nicole, and my grandchildren Corrina & Jakob; for whom there are no limits.
- Jim Gentile

To my wife Ann & son Matt, who gave me the two best reasons imaginable to take life seriously, and to my old pals for reminding me not to. And to Bro Ken, who had a gift for finding the humor in everything.
- Russell Slocum

Introduction

Legend has it that 5000 or so years ago, a sagacious Chinese emperor named Fu Hsi used tortoise shell markings to derive a set of symbols that, in various combinations, served as divine guidance for dealing with times of change. Around 1500 B.C., this philosophical system was scratched onto oxbone, and The *I Ching* began its run as one of the most popular and enduring texts in history.

On par with the Bible and the Koran, *The I Ching: A Book of Changes* is the foundation of Eastern thought. It is considered a sacred text among the Chinese, the common root for Taoism and Confucianism, and a valued guide for followers of Buddhism. There are countless translations, interpretations and derivations.

The Bit Ching Book of Change may be radically Westernized and a little irreverent, but its intention is a faithful update of the original - to offer guidance for overcoming the fear, anger, and uncertainty within us, as well as the morons, pitfalls and other obstacles around us. In an age and business environment too often typified by greed, aggression and betrayal, it shows how the virtues at the heart of Eastern philosophy, such as awareness, adaptability, openness, perseverance, restraint and balance, still can be used to define and achieve success.

Much of this book relates to building a career, but readers may find that most of these perspectives are analogous to non-business situations as well. As a whole, the book is more about defining and attaining your individual idea of success, and dealing with the people and challenges that can help or hinder you in the pursuit.

The Bit Ching Book of Change uses the same 64 symbolic hexagrams (aka kuas) as the *I Ching*, but makes three significant departures from the classic structure:

1. *Consultation of the Kuas*: Traditionally, to determine which of the 64 hexagramic kuas in *The I Ching* should be consulted, the reader tosses a set of three coins or yarrow stalks six times. The resulting 6-line symbol (a combination of two trigrams) on a chart refers the tosser to the appropriate reading for divining one's future.

   This requires patience, discipline, and faith that a Higher Force is guiding each toss. With all due respect for the wisdom of the ancient readings, *The Bit Ching* takes a faster approach. We figure that a challenge occurs when an external situation or force is met with uncertainty or otherwise conflicting emotions. So we replaced the traditional symbols of Sky, Thunder, River, etc., with a grid of Outer Forces and Inner Forces. You'll find this grid inside the front and back covers. To seek the solution to the challenge, just see where the forces intersect and go to that chapter.

2. *Order of the Hexagrams*: Around 1100 B.C., a scholar-governor named Wen combined two popular versions of *The I Ching* into a new interpretation and changed the order of the hexagrams. Most versions since then have kept Wen's order. We reordered the hexagrams again, this time into chapters of similar situations, giving readers the convenient option to poke around nearby chapters for related perspectives.

3. *Parables*: For each hexagram, *The I Ching* offers advice in a general reading, followed by specifics for each line that was created by tossing all heads or all tails. Instead of this line item guidance, *The Bit Ching* offers a modern parable set somewhat in the style of the *Analects of Confucius*, but featuring the wisdom and actions of one Working Dog.

About Working Dog

The character of Working Dog is based on my coauthor, Jim Gentile. The brief stories accompanying the 64 chapters in this book are simplified to the style of little parables, but they're all essentially true examples of how Jim applied principles of the I Ching to accomplish goals in his business and personal life.

Jim has been a fan of Eastern philosophy in general, and the I Ching in particular, since he was twenty. He credits much of his personal growth and business accomplishments to its teachings, which add interesting facets to his bawdy, no-bullshit style.

And he has accomplished much. Starting with a modest upbringing in a working class family, a two-year degree in engineering, and no money, Jim turned passions for people and building into a construction management company and a portfolio of over 500 commercial buildings and projects from Houston to Boston, most in the Mid-Atlantic region. He is one of those hyper-productive individuals who might mention an idea, ("You know, it might be interesting to..."), and when you see him a few weeks later, he's seen it, done it, or in the process of building it. He and his wife Denise were charmed by the island of St. John in the US Virgin Islands. Tune in a couple years later, and he has built their own island stone mountaintop villa overlooking a quiet bay. As of this writing, Jim owns all or part of a construction company, a property development company, two medical centers, a retirement community and various industrial parks and other commercial properties.

Not that success should be defined by a list of assets. To quote chapter 16 herein, "Many people get the superficial trappings of success by screwing others. That doesn't make them successful. That just makes them assholes with a lot of money." What is notable is that Jim has attained success by common measure while doing right by others. He counts hundreds of customers as eager references. He is equally proud of being an inventor, songwriter, musician, philosopher, father and grandfather, as well as friend and confidante to many.

Usually sporting a beard, jeans, dirty boots and a similarity to how Jerry Garcia might have looked if he'd stayed off junk food and junk, Jim Gentile is not the cover model for GQ's dress-for-success issue. The fact that he obviously couldn't care less is part of his charisma. His outgoing nature and contagious belly laugh tend to put people at ease and pull them together, whether they're in a corporate boardroom or a Caribbean beach bar.

Meeting Jim, you probably wouldn't sense his devotion to ancient Eastern philosophy, at least at first. But seeing how he handles situations and interacts with others, it connects. This balance is the spirit of The Bit Ching Book of Change.

-Russell Slocum

Table of Contents

V. HANDLING MORONS

VI. WINNING OTHERS OVER

VII. LEADING WISELY

VIII. HANDLING SUCCESS

I. CONFRONTING OBSTACLES

Time's going by like an old freight train
You keep singing that same old refrain
Someday you'll wonder what happened to life
Someday you'll get caught in the rain.

It's all up to you,
There are no excuses
Ideals are so useless
When it's time to be real.

  Lyrics from Time to Be Real,
  By James Gentile

During a golf outing, The Customer sliced his shot. They found his ball lying in the middle of a small, shallow creek. He tried to reach the ball from the bank, but could not. He jumped across a narrower part of the creek and tried from the other side, and still could not.

"I can't get my ball," The Customer sighed.

"Sure you can," observed Working Dog. "You just aren't willing to pay the price."

1. SHI HE / Biting through the obstacle
(*Obstacle/Overload*)

"Can't" usually means "won't"

When you speak of your limitation or burden, you misuse the word "can't." What you mean to say is "won't." Virtually anything is possible; what you mean to say is that you are unwilling to pay the price. Look again at what you must sacrifice if you wish to achieve your goal. Then you can proceed accepting what is at stake, or dismiss the notion and move on.

Working Dog was trying to play catch with his young daughter, but with every throw the young girl recoiled.

"What are you afraid of?" asked Working Dog.

"I'm afraid the ball will hit me, and I'll get hurt," she replied.

Working Dog picked up the ball. As they walked toward the house, Working Dog threw the ball at The Daughter, just hard enough to sting her arm.

"OW!" she cried. "Why did you do that?"

"Did it hurt?" he asked.

"Yes!"

"Does it still hurt?" he asked.

After a moment, she replied, "No."

"If that's the worst that can happen, is it worth being afraid of it?"

They resumed their catch, and The Daughter was less afraid.

2. K'AN / The Abyss
(*Obstacle/Apprehension*)

One way to fail: fear of trying

Don't take idiotic chances, but ask yourself whether fear of losing is what is discouraging you from trying. Define what you fear. What is the worst that can happen? If you lose money, you can make it back. If you get bruised, you'll heal. What will others think if you don't succeed? Who cares?

Living is like juggling: if you think too much about what you are doing, you lose your balls. When you worry, you do not perform well, and fears become self-fulfilling. Consider all of the things that you've feared. How many actually happened? Very, very few. And those that did were probably never as bad as you imagined they'd be.

Even if you lose something tangible, you will also lose your fear as part of the process. Yet some people hang onto their misery as if they are afraid of losing it. Don't dwell in the past or make excuses. It's your life, and it's up to you alone to make the most of it. There's neither time nor place for fear of failure.

When Working Dog's construction business was only a few years old, the building industry came to a standstill. Banks stopped lending money. Customers could not pay Working Dog, and no new work was coming in.

On their way to a martial arts camp for a weekend retreat, Working Dog told his wife that when they returned from the retreat, he was going to close the business.

"You will do what you must," she said.

At the camp, Working Dog funneled his frustration into energy, which seemed boundless. In the middle of an exercise, The Instructor stopped everyone.

"As long as you push yourself and try your best, and give the effort like this man is giving, you can never fail," said The Instructor. It was as if he saw all of the frustrations and issues that were being channeled into Working Dog's actions.

The light that went on in Working Dog's mind continued to brighten through the session. When it was over, Working Dog told his wife. "I'm not quitting."

"You will do what you must," she said.

𝟑. TUN / Obstacles at the outset
(*Obstacle/Frustration*)

The other way to fail: quit

If you keep trying, and keep doing the best you can, you won't fail until you quit. If you hang in long enough to succeed, people will praise your perseverance. If you stop short of that, they will say that you were stupid to try. If you don't have a passion for what you do, you won't persevere.

The solution is simple: do something you love, work toward a realistic goal, and don't quit. Get knocked down, get back up...

Working Dog received a frantic call from one of his daughters, who was nearing the end of her last semester of college.

"I'm totally overwhelmed," cried The Daughter. "I have so much to do that I can't do anything. I'll never get it all done!"

After calming his daughter, Working Dog had her detail all of the papers she needed to write, tests for which she needed to study, and other responsibilities. Working Dog wrote down all of the tasks.

"Which is due first, and when?" he asked. After she told him, they went down the rest of the list, discussing each project's scope and due date.

"You can do it all if you follow just two rules," said Working Dog. "First, I want you to concentrate on only one project at a time. While you're working on it, the other projects don't exist. Don't worry about them, don't keep track of them. I'll do that. Second, call me each day, and I'll tell you what to do next."

The two spoke every day during the next weeks. The Daughter completed her coursework, and graduated knowing the difference between managing a schedule and being managed by one.

4. XIAO CH'U / A long journey made of many small steps
(*Obstacle/Distraction*)

Slow down to speed up

You have set your sights on a long-term objective, but you tend to think about all the things you have to do to get there, and you want to do them all at once. When you look only at the large picture, you overwhelm yourself before you begin. Instead, break it down and take one step at a time.

The end goal must always be in the back of your mind. But between here and that point, there are many waypoints, shorter-term goals to pass through on your way. Focus on these. Revisit your long-term goal only occasionally, when it is time to step back and make sure that you are still on course.

The Sensei at the Tae Kwon Do camp divided the 150 students into three empires, gave each a different colored armband, and arranged the groups in a triangle in the field.

"I have chosen the three highest black belts to lead the empires," explained The Sensei. "Follow their orders. At my signal, open battle will begin. When you lose a point, you must assume the victors' colors and join their side. Be prepared for a long battle. It will not be over until there is only one empire."

The leaders were given several minutes to prepare their strategies. The leader of the empire to which Working Dog was assigned expressed concern.

"I may be a good fighter, but I know my weaknesses, and I know I am not a leader," the Black Belt said to Working Dog, who was a blue belt at the time. "You may be a lower belt, but I know you are a good leader. What would be your strategy?"

Working Dog divided their entire empire into pairs of fighters. "You have only two jobs," he said. "Protect each other, and do only what I tell you."

Upon The Sensei's signal, the other two empires immediately converged upon each other in a confused battle. Working Dog's empire stood in place. As defeated fighters from the other armies straggled from the melee to don their new colors, Working Dog would send a pair of his fighters to pick them off. Within a half hour, they had taken over both other empires.

"In all my years teaching, I have never seen anything like this," exclaimed The Sensei. "Rather than exposing all of your troops to one big battle, you used them tactically in many little battles. I too have learned something today."

∫. SHI / The Army
(Bullshit/Overload)

Break it down, or it will break you down

The analytical mind is powerful for planning. Virtually anything is doable and manageable when you break it down. Analyze the situation, break it down to the necessary tasks, and prioritize them. Then turn off your analytical mind and its tendency to want to do everything at once; it will only be in the way. Address and delegate the tasks individually. Stick to your plan, but remain flexible enough to adjust your priorities, because they will change. Unanticipated twists and turns will arise; these are not dead-ends, just part of the course.

In order to make it possible for The Customer to afford the recording studio of his dreams, Working Dog had agreed to own the structure in partnership with The Banker, and rent it to The Customer.

The studio was built and equipped to be one of the best in world. They could do practically everything: original music, remixes, sound tracks, commercials, films and videos. But after a strong beginning, the studio's business soured. Working Dog renegotiated to ease the customer's burden as much as possible, and accepted promises of money forthcoming. But whenever he visited the studio, Working Dog seldom saw anyone working except a well-known freelance producer who was renting one of the recording spaces, and never saw any of the money promised.

"We're screwed," said The Banker in frustration. "They'll never be able to pay us what they owe. We'll have to throw them out, sell the equipment at a discount to recover a fraction of our money, and lease the building to someone else."

"Let's not panic," said Working Dog. He approached The Producer and asked for his opinion on why the business had failed.

"Part of it is personalities," said The Producer, "but another problem was that they were trying to be all things to all people."

Working Dog laid out his plan to focus only on the music industry, and invited The Producer to work with him. Within a month from the time that he had decided to act, Working Dog was in the recording business, with some of the best connections, equipment and buzz in the industry.

6. WEI JI / Before Completion
(*Obstacle/Confusion*)

Make stumbling blocks into steppingstones

In every obstacle there is a challenge, and in every challenge there is opportunity. Be patient, but not timid. When faced with challenge characterized by disorder, act decisively, but not rashly. Get the situation in perspective, gather your energy, wait for the right moment, and then move swiftly. Stumbling blocks can be steppingstones when they are in the right place and you use them wisely.

Nine contractors had been invited to present proposals for the office complex. Eight of them wore suits, presented charts, and said nearly the same thing. The exception was Working Dog. His boots were dirty, his style was casual, and he joked often through his presentation.

Working Dog was one of two contractors that The Customer called for a follow-up meeting.

"Didn't you feel like you should be like the others in order to level the playing field?" asked The Customer.

"Since you'll practically be living with the contractor you select for the next six months, I felt you should see who I really am," said Working Dog. "If the others all seem the same, any one of them will do. If my approach is different and you like it, I automatically have half of the playing field."

7. K'UN / Yielding
(*Obstacle/Ego*)

Accept who you are...

A good way to make a fool of yourself is to try to impress upon people that you aren't one. You earn trust and respect by being yourself, not who you think people want you to be.

The most cost-efficient type of building is a box: square corners, no wasted space or extra effort. It is also the most boring type of building. Character is shown in people as it is in architecture, by peculiar inefficiencies and unusual qualities. As long as they don't compromise your effectiveness, accept the quirks in your personality as a design bonus.

Be proud of your work and of yourself. But do not be vain about it. Take your work seriously, not your self.

Working Dog and a real estate broker had been discussing the habit of local governments to spend money and efforts on wooing out-of-state businesses, but doing little to help or keep the companies that were already there. The Broker left for a meeting, but a short time later an idea occurred to Working Dog. Although he preferred talking directly to others rather than emailing, the builder sent his idea to The Broker: Construct identical buildings on each side of the river separating the two states. Move half of the operation into each, with each half set up as a separate company. Every two years, each half will tell the other state that you'll move there for incentives and tax breaks. Move your business, wait a couple years, then strike the same deal to move back. Repeat this every two years. It's a stroke of genius.

An hour later The Broker called. "It IS a stroke of genius," he said. "Your problem is that you can't spell for shit. Your email said it was a stroke of 'guines.' Keep coming up with ideas, but just don't try to write them down all by yourself."

From that time on, The Broker called Working Dog "The Guiness."

JIAN / Smooth, gradual development
(*Obstacle/Resignation*)

...but never stop striving to improve

You can change or overcome anything you truly want to, but be selective, because change has a price. Be aware of who you are. Recognize your strong points and build on them. Recognize your weak points, but don't spend too much time working on them unless they are truly compromising. The best that you'll usually do is neutralize your weaknesses. If that is your main focus, you are aspiring to mediocrity. When you are not good at something, ally yourself with people who are better at it, and let them do it.

II. GETTING YOUR BEARINGS

Fill your heart with love and laughter.
Pain and sorrow, let it be.
Comes a time when all's forgotten.
Live your life and set it free.

Should have known it won't be easy.
Should have known it will be hard.
Time will come when life will guide you
Through the gateway in your heart.

*Lyrics from **Should Have Known**,*
By Michael P. Feiner & James Gentile

During their first trip to Asia, Working Dog and his wife stayed several days at a large hotel in Hanoi. Few Americans were there. According to the concierge, most of the rooms were filled with visiting government officials.

Early one morning Working Dog left the hotel for a walk. As usual, the street was lined with 3-wheeled cyclos, their drivers sitting on the curbs awaiting passengers or goods to transport. As Working Dog approached the corner, a fast-moving cyclo piled high with bundles of fabric tipped over, spilling its cargo into the busy intersection. Working Dog dodged the traffic that continued to bustle past the accident, and helped the driver right the cart. The two men worked feverishly to pile the material back in place. As he secured the last bundle onto the cart, Working Dog heard applause. He had not noticed that the cyclo drivers waiting by the hotel had stood from their roosts on the curb, along with many pedestrians who had stopped to observe the unusual sight. Dozens of people were smiling and clapping as Working Dog grinned and bowed in return, and oblivious government officials weaved through the crowd on the way to their meetings.

_9_. CUI / Selective gathering
(_Interaction/Confusion_)

First sweep your own porch

It is important to give back, to help others. But joining a group or cause is not a wise first step. You cannot help others until you take care of yourself. Start by sweeping your own porch. When that is clean, help your neighbors sweep theirs. Reach out to the people around you. When your street is clean, help the other people in your life. If everyone did just this, the world would shine.

One evening, as he was returning to his office after dinner, Working Dog met The Architect, who was leaving his neighboring building for the day.

"The industry is slow," observed The Architect. "How is it that your business is so good that you must work nights?"

"For years, my car was the last to leave the parking lot every night," replied Working Dog. "I'm now working late because we are busy, but we are busy because I have been working late."

1⊙. SUI / The flow toward to the truth
(*Crossroads/Distraction*)

Choose and follow your path

Don't count on a wealthy relative or divine intervention to plop you into a corner office; the respect and success that you will earn in your career will be proportionate to the effort that you invest in it. It is remarkable how few exceptions there are to this correlation. It is even more remarkable how many people don't accept it.

Be honest about what you are willing to sacrifice in order to achieve your long-term career goal. There are three paths of commitment. Your journey takes shape when you choose one, accept it as a guiding truth, then go with its flow.

Path 1: A Job
Perhaps your highest priority is spending every possible moment with your family or hobby. Perhaps you have a low threshold for pressure. There's nothing wrong with promptly punching out after your eight hours, providing while you're at work you do the best that you can.

Path 2: A Career
If you want a professional career being something other than a bureaucrat, you cannot expect to leave your job every day at 5:00. You need to commit to excelling at what you do, assume a higher level of accountability than the baseline requires, and continually look for opportunities to improve your company and your personal performance.

Path 3: A Business
The highest level, assuming ownership of a business, can be literal or figurative. It may actually be your own business, but it can also mean the total commitment to managing a department, project or otherwise finite responsibility. Treat it as if it were your own business, assume total accountability for its health and future, and give without hesitation all of the time and attention it will demand.

"There's a lot of work to be done," Working Dog said to his wife as the family ate dinner.

"Does this mean we won't see you?" worried one of The Daughters.

"You will see me most nights for dinner," promised Working Dog, "and we'll plan what we're going to do together every weekend."

The Daughters happily greeted their father every night. Although he usually returned to the office after he kissed them goodnight, and spent every Sunday night planning the next week's work, the time the family spent together was rich and rewarding.

11. JIA RÊN / Family
(Crossroads/Overload)

You can succeed in business AND put your family first, if...

...and only if your family will put YOU first. Your family must understand and truly appreciate that they are living and growing with your business, and getting opportunities that they otherwise would not. If they can accept that you will not be around as often as the bureaucrat down the street, the relationship will work, and the time that you can give to them can be happy, not rife with resentment. They need not just to endure your commitment, but support it. If they cannot, or if you cannot reciprocate, something will break.

"There is no place on the island for tradesmen like me to stay," griped The Stonemason, who came south to work for several months each winter. Working Dog noted an opportunity to develop an apartment complex at the other end of the short ferry route, where land on the larger island was cheaper.

"It's hard to find anything down here, even the materials we need," chimed The Plumber, and The Electrician agreed. Working Dog figured he could establish a one-person purchasing office on the mainland to coordinate orders with an agent on the island, and every week ship a container of supplies needed by local contractors.

When he got home, Working Dog found that the electricity on that part of the island had gone off again. From the veranda, looking out over the sea, he wondered how much energy a grid of sea fan generators could harness from the tides.

12. QIAN / Creative force
(Crossroads/Confusion)

Opportunity is everywhere

Don't start a business endeavor hoping that, "If I build it, they will come." It is much easier to start where the customers are already lined up.

Wherever there is a need unfulfilled, there is opportunity. Be aware. Ask questions. Listen to the answers. People complain constantly about not being able to get something that they want. In every gripe there is a potential opportunity. Select one that appeals to your aptitude and attitude, then be creative. Devise a way to fill the void, and deliver the solution.

Working Dog was somewhat surprised when The Processor told him that he had been awarded the contract to build the new plant. Three other companies had bid on the project, two of which had much more experience in constructing food processing plants.

"That's fantastic," said Working Dog. After they had discussed the next steps, he inquired, "May I ask why you chose me?"

"My business may seem pretty boring to some people, but I love what I do," said The Processor. "Out of all the construction companies I met with, you were the only one who seemed to truly love what you do. I appreciate the value of working with someone who'll not just put his mind into my project, but put his heart into it as well."

13. Yü / Enthusiasm
(*Obstacle/Greed*)

Pursue your passion

Match your appetite with your aptitude. Consider what your passion is, and how you can make a career of it. When you know where you want to be, work constantly toward that point.

Choose your career for passion, not profit. If you have complete passion for what you are doing, you will meet each day with pride and purpose. Share that passion with your customers, and the money will come. You spend around 120 hours a week awake. If you are serious about your business, you will spend at least half of those hours at it. If you don't enjoy what you are doing, and are working only for the money, the days will be long and the years will be short as you waste half of your life.

The Customer could barely control his enthusiasm. "I have a fantastic idea for another business," he told Working Dog, who had constructed three manufacturing plants for The Customer. "You know how I love working on hot rods. There is nowhere around here to get parts. I can make a lot of money with a store specializing in this."

"First of all, you already make a lot of money in your manufacturing business," noted Working Dog. "Secondly, do you love working on your cars, or do you love the idea of selling auto parts? If you make a business of it, you will block your escape route."

14. DA GUO / Great pressure
(*Crossroads/Resignation*)

Find two passions

If you are truly passionate about your business, it will be easy to get absorbed by it. You might proudly tell people, "I worked 100 hours last week." In time, you will realize how stupid this sounds, and that who you are has become indistinguishable from what you do. If your only passion is for your work, it will become an obsession and eventually cease to be fun.

The harder you work, the more important it is to find something outside of it to help you keep your balance. Embrace a second passion, such as family, fishing, woodworking or playing music, something that you genuinely enjoy and that you reserve for your personal life. This counterbalance will help you clear your head, maintain your perspective and enjoy both interests to their fullest. No matter how much you work, you don't have time not to have fun.

"Who has taught you the most about your business?" asked The Customer.

Working Dog named the owner of a large construction company where he had worked for two years. "He divided his employees between the office and the field, and set up rivalries to keep them polarized and under his control," recalled Working Dog. "He had everyone focusing on volume, bringing in as many dollars as possible instead of looking at the profitability. And instead of paying the subcontractors on time, he would string them out as long as possible, and ignore their phone calls."

"Didn't he go out of business?" asked The Customer.

"Of course he did," said Working Dog. "But not until he taught me many important things not to do."

15. YI / Increase
(*Crossroads/Ego*)

Learn only from your own experience, and you will die stupid

Experience is the best teacher, but life is a relatively short class. If you rely solely on your own experience for wisdom, you will die stupid.

There is as much to learn from watching others do things poorly as from watching them do things well. When you find good, imitate it. When you find familiar faults in others, correct them in yourself. When you see where others err, avoid it. Remembering where others go wrong is a shortcut that you shouldn't miss.

Wherever you are, you are surrounded by fertile fields for growing your knowledge. Everyone knows something that you do not. If you develop an enthusiasm for learning from others, no matter how dull or odd people may seem, you will find that they know something that can enlighten or benefit you in some way. Find out what their passions are, and encourage people to talk about them. You'll find that you actually inspire them by showing interest in something dear to them, because few others ever will. By merely asking questions, you will find yourself regarded as a brilliant conversationalist. Giving and getting in this manner can be one of the most gratifying things in life.

"What is your dream?" Working Dog asked The Applicant.

"I would like to be driven around every day in a big limousine, and have everyone look up to me," replied The Applicant.

"Do you have any idea how you'd get the money to afford the limo?" continued Working Dog.

"I don't know," said The Applicant. "Whatever it takes to succeed."

"From what I've seen, success is more about taking pride in what you do, doing something you enjoy and doing it well," said Working Dog. "This comes from earning the trust and respect of those around you, and helping them achieve their goals and dreams as well. It's not how much money you have, or the size of your house or car. Many people get the superficial trappings of success by screwing others. That doesn't make them successful. That just makes them assholes with a lot of money."

16. GUI MEI / The Enchantress
(*Crossroads/Greed*)

Keep money in perspective

In business, success is usually equated with wealth. That is how most people keep score, and financial success often provides credibility that in turn brings in more work. Make money part of the game, but not the ultimate goal.

Money can be an enchanting seductress and bring pleasures and possessions, but it is an inaccurate barometer of happiness. Peel away the thickest layers of possessions from people who compulsively surround themselves with such things, and you will often find an empty spirit. There are proportionately as many miserable wealthy people as there are miserable people of average means. Perhaps even more.

If you work just for money, it will taint your decisions, and you won't truly be happy with your work or yourself. The two earmarks of a satisfying career – whether your job is building a business or raising a family – are not fame and fortune; they are pride and purpose. Pursue a passion in which you find gratification, put that above the financial rewards, and you will feel that you always have enough money. Place money first, and you will feel that you never have enough.

III: RENEWING YOUR SPIRIT

Caught in the current,
gotta have you near.
The water's all around me,
can't afford the fear.
It's the thrill that keeps me going,
and the pace that wears me out.
Gotta keep on going,
can't afford the doubt.

        *Lyrics from **Old River Flow**,*
        By James Gentile

When he started his business, Working Dog managed the construction while his partner assumed responsibility for the business side of the company. Their first customer was a young doctor, starting his own practice with a new building. The project went well, but Working Dog's partner soon proved to have neither the contacts nor financial backing that he promised to bring to the relationship, and he and Working Dog parted ways.

Several years later, Working Dog got a panicked call from the same doctor. "I hired your ex-partner to build another medical center for me, and the guy is driving me nuts," said The Doctor. "He's all talk, he never follows through with anything. I need your help."

"I wish I could help," replied Working Dog regretfully, "but he and I aren't in business anymore." However Working Dog made some suggestions as to how The Doctor could keep the project and ex-partner on track, and eventually the job was completed.

Two years later, The Doctor hired Working Dog for a third medical center, and the project went swiftly and flawlessly. They worked together many times after that, and with each time, The Doctor became less involved in the construction, confident that Working Dog would always deliver on promises.

One day a dozen people were gathered in a conference room to launch The Doctor's most ambitious project yet – the state's first freestanding surgery center. The Doctor stood and pointed to Working Dog.

"He knows what I want," said The Doctor, and left the room.

17. LIN / Approaching
(*Pressure/Resignation*)

If you always go halfway, you'll never get there.

Doing the best that you possibly can with every job may seem like the hard way, but it is ultimately the easy way. When you commit to doing something, do it thoroughly. There are no acceptable levels less than what you promised. Occasionally there may be reasons why you might not be able to deliver 100%. But these are not excuses, nor should they be acceptable to you or others.

At work, you lay the groundwork for success when you understand that the purpose of your business is to make part of your customers' lives easier or otherwise better for them. Do the best possible job that you can with everything you do, every time, and your reputation will grow. People will call you for work, and pay you what you are worth. They will do this gladly because they know that there will be no hassles, no excuses.

A year after he had finished construction of the assisted living center, Working Dog still hadn't been paid. His phone calls to The Developers were ignored. Many of the rooms were still vacant, and the community was not being marketed or maintained. Working Dog contacted the three other investors, who expressed similar frustration.

Posing as a potential buyer, Working Dog approached The Developers' accounting firm. When he examined the books, he found no accounting of the debt or the money they had taken from HUD and evidently used elsewhere. They were lying to everyone. Looking deeper into their past, Working Dog found that this wasn't the first time these developers had cheated others.

Working Dog approached them with the facts, and said he and the other investors would either take it over or prosecute. The Developers' handed over the property.

Working Dog worked intensely to get the facility and business side running smoothly, but neither he nor the other honest investors had the qualifications or desire to manage the community. Working Dog looked for someone who did, and found a father and son who had the experience and dream for doing exactly that, although they were uneasy about shouldering the financial responsibilities alone. They worked out a deal, putting in enough of their own money to buy out the other investors, and sharing ownership with Working Dog, who helped bring the place back up to the initial quality, then stepped away to let the father and son run it. Within a year, the community was full and regarded as one of the nicest in the valley. The partners meet once a quarter to discuss community news and needs, and how to share the profits.

18. GUAI / Resolve
(*Pressure/Frustration*)

You gotta wanna

You compound pressure and frustration by not being totally committed to what you are doing. Major goals are achieved through an extended process. If the prospect of reaching that goal does not outweigh the sacrifices involved in the process, you won't have the resolve to stay with it. Ensure a sustainable balance by choosing a goal that genuinely appeals to your heart, and a process that is enjoyable. This will give you the resolve to see it through the hurdles you face.

Trying to get approval to construct a new medical center, Working Dog confronted a new obstacle at every turn. Nearby homeowners had fought previous efforts to develop the land, but Working Dog won them over. Townships that shared the land had squabbled over the sewer and taxes for years, but Working Dog negotiated an agreement. Government agencies had questioned the environmental impact, but Working Dog proved their concerns unfounded.

The last hurdle for approval was the ability to add more lanes to the narrow access strip that connected the lot to the main road. Another developer held the option to buy one side of that strip, but he demanded a ridiculous price to which none of the investing doctors would or should agree. On the other side was a Retailer who said he wanted to be a good neighbor, but repeatedly found reasons not to sell several unused feet of land that Working Dog needed. This persisted for months, until a township meeting when The Retailer finally revealed his true feelings.

"The project will congest traffic around my store," objected The Retailer. "It's a bad idea, and the township should never approve it."

Working Dog left the meeting feeling that months of work had been wasted. Without the ability to widen the access road, the project would die. But Working Dog took a deeper look at everything, and found one possibility. The other developer would undoubtedly exercise his right to renew his option to buy the parcel, but technically that option ran out in a week.

Working Dog approached the owner of the parcel, described his project, and asked him if he would be willing to sell the land.

"That developer has jerked me around for years," said The Parcel Owner. "I'd be happy to sell it to you."

At dawn on the day that The Developer's option expired, Working Dog acquired the parcel, and his project moved forward.

19. K'UN / Oppression
(*Pressure/Overload*)

Where there's burnout, there's still a spark

Just as there have been times when everything went right for you, there are times when your life seems like the cosmic dumping ground for misfortune. When obstacles pile up, it becomes a wall that can make you feel trapped, depressed, exhausted and emotionally drained. If you give in to despair, you will let yourself be buried. Don't cave in.

Look within yourself and you will find a spark, enough faith in your strength and resolve to keep your spirit alive. By this light, try to distance yourself from the adverse circumstances so you can look at them objectively. Although a path out may not be immediately apparent, if you persevere it eventually will take shape, and you will find the way.

Working Dog and his friend carefully followed the guidelines of each of the dozen publishers to whom they submitted their manuscript, but during the next several months, nearly all returned it apparently unread and covered with an unsigned, all-purpose rejection slip. At one publishing house, the manuscript climbed several levels, but nearly a year later it too was returned.

"It's a good book, but how can we sell it when nobody knows who you are?" explained The Editor.

"I guess I'll either have to kill somebody or find another way," observed Working Dog.

It took him and The Friend a couple days to research the printing and distribution processes, enlist graphic designers and a printer, and detail the plan to manage their own production. In less time than it took most of the publishing houses to transfer the original submission to the self-addressed, stamped envelope, the book was nearly ready to go to press.

2⊙. HÊNG / Persevering
(Pressure/Distraction)

For every action, there is a distraction

You can always find a reason not to do something. You are not alone. Negative people instinctively conjure obstacles and fearful prospects for proposed action. Positive people are easily lured off course by grander or more exciting notions. In the course of any endeavor, there will be countless temptations not to complete it as planned.

This is why perseverance will enable you to stand out. Once you set a goal and direction, stick to it. An ambitious effort needs to be taken one step at a time. Conditions will change, and you will have to adjust your course as you go. Between each step, fix again on your objective, and renew your effort. But the difference between distraction and focused reaction will be the difference between failure and success.

Working Dog was writing and recording a song for his parents, and invited The Guitarist to work on the lead while Working Dog sang and played the rhythm. The Guitarist created a complex, overpowering score that was technically superb, but had little feeling.

That night Working Dog went through the tape, and removed many of the notes that The Guitarist had played. The next day, he played the edited tape for The Guitarist.

"That's beautiful," said The Guitarist. "Are you sure that was what I played?"

"That is you playing, and I think it was what you wanted to play," said Working Dog. "The problem was that you filled all the voids. It's the spaces as much as the notes that give music heart. If you fill all of the voids, you have no room left for feeling. When you play is just as important as what you play."

21. DUN / Time to step back
(*Pressure/Apprehension*)

A mind is a terrible thing to use...

...when you use it to revisit repeatedly the same information. Analytical thinking can be indispensable when it is strategically applied, debilitating when it runs through the same information excessively and without purpose. Reprocessing quickly turns to worry. When you find yourself doing this, list everything you must do on a piece of paper and prioritize the tasks. Then do the first thing and withdraw from the rest, putting them out of your mind. When people say that they are "multitasking," what they really mean is that they are bouncing back and forth between two things because they can't decide which is more important.

...when you use it to overanalyze. Once you have all of the relevant facts, trust your gut. Beauty often lies in simplicity, and your mind has a natural desire to fill in voids to understand things as deeply as possible. When your mind tries to manipulate every technical detail of something, it is easy to lose sight of its heart. Step back, and the view will be clearer.

"How many people were at the concert last night?" asked The Partner.

"A couple hundred, I'd say," said Working Dog.

"That's odd," said The Partner. "I thought it was sold out months ago."

"It was," said Working Dog. "In fact, there were 20,000 bodies in the audience. However, all but a couple hundred spent the entire evening waving one hand in the air, with their cell phones in the other hand. "

22. LV / Walking
(*Pressure/Confusion*)

Be where you are

Your mind is most useful when it is in the same place as your body. Focus on the immediate, the step you are now taking. If you are thinking about things other than the task or experience at hand, you are diluting the effort, efficiency or pleasure of the moment.

If you proceed on your path with awareness and self-discipline, life can be relatively easy. Notice how people around you make it hard by overwhelming themselves with distractions and worries, and then complaining about having too much to do. If your mind is somewhere else, you're ill equipped to make the best of what is at hand. And that's no one's fault but yours.

"I won't make a final decision before my lawyer meets you," said The Customer. "But if he feels the same way I do, we'll have a deal." They arranged for everyone to meet the next day at The Customer's office.

Working Dog walked into the room where the two other men waited. As they were introduced, Working Dog feigned concern and said to The Customer, "I have to tell you, there might be a conflict of interest here."

"What is it?" asked The Customer. "Do you two know each other?"

"No," said Working Dog, "but we're kind of related. I'm a fucking contractor, and he's a fucking lawyer."

"Hire him," laughed The Attorney.

23. JING / The Well
(*Pressure/Ego*)

Keep it fun

You have a sense of humor; make it part of the way you do business, another resource that others can draw upon. Keep your manner professional yet lighthearted, and those around your will respond in kind. People work better when they are having a good time.

You will strengthen your leadership by cultivating an environment where dedication to work and an enjoyable workplace are not mutually exclusive virtues. Establish a culture that encourages fun, while holding sacred the quality of work and the pride that people take in it, and you will counter the tendency for people to associate having fun with not taking the work seriously.

A workplace that includes fun exudes a vitality that customers notice and appreciate. If all else is equal, the customer will choose to work with the people who will make the experience more enjoyable.

The subcontractors were uneasy as Working Dog walked around the construction area, saying nothing.

"What's the matter?" asked The Foreman nervously.

"There are piles of crap all over. This is a hospital and it looks like a dump. Tell everyone to clean up their shit," said Working Dog calmly. He then left to meet with the doctors who had hired him.

As the meeting with the doctors came to a close, a group of nurses asked if they could take a peek at the work area. Working Dog was confident that the subcontractors had enough time to clean up, so he agreed to let the nurses in.

As he opened the door, he saw a large banner that The Foreman had hung on the wall. It said: CLEAN UP YOUR SHIT!

The laughter of the nurses reminded Working Dog that if you are direct and keep a sense of humor, not many situations are awkward.

24. SUN / Decrease
(Interaction/Ego)

Use humor to defuse problems

Put your ego aside and confront your challenge rationally and, if possible, with humor.

Laugh often. In this way, when you are upset with something, you do not need to yell. All you need to do is not laugh, and others will understand that there is something wrong that must be remedied.

IV: CUTTING THE BULLSHIT

You always take the easy way,
You don't wanna make it hard.
You're always dealing from the bottom
Cause you don't wanna play your card.

When you really wanna play it
Then deal me in.
But don't try to bluff me,
Cause you don't wanna know where I've been.

> *Lyrics from **You Don't Wanna Know**,*
> *By Don Consul & James Gentile*

All summer, Working Dog had tried unsuccessfully to meet with booking agents to get a gig for his band. As autumn approached, he went directly to the clubs, but the managers also were too busy to hear his music. He met other musicians, who agreed that the system was cliquish and unfair.

"But that's the way it is," they lamented.

Working Dog called the owner of a summer playhouse. "Your theater stays closed all winter," said Working Dog. "Let my group put on a concert. I will organize and promote the event, and split the profits with you. You simply turn on the heat and open the doors."

The concert sold out. After the performance, the elated Theater Owner asked Working Dog if he had any other ideas.

"Why not hold a concert here every month during the winter?" suggested Working Dog. "I will organize and promote all of the events, and you and the musicians can split the profits."

Working Dog was soon sought after by the booking agents, who also expressed new eagerness to hear his music. The Theater Owner enjoyed a successful winter, while Working Dog played wherever he wished.

𝟤𝟧. **P'I** / Stagnation
(*Bullshit/Resignation*)

"The way it is" isn't

You do not have to accept the situation. You have choices for practically everything in life, and your world is built from the ones you make. Most of those decisions carry a price tag, something else that you will have to do or sacrifice in return. Be aware that you always have choices, weigh their price, and act. Whatever you do, what you become, is almost entirely up to you.

While he was in college, Working Dog worked nights and weekends at a department store to help pay his expenses. For months he had tried to join the store's union to make the same wages as other workers, but the union put him off time after time.

Shortly after announcing that they would soon be going on strike, The Union Rep greeted Working Dog with the papers to join.

"For months I asked you to join, but you jerked me around, and you cost me a lot of money," replied Working Dog. "Now you want me stand on a picket line with you, which will cost me even more money. No way."

On the first day of the strike, several picketers tried to block Working Dog's way into the store. Working Dog got a baseball bat from his car, and asked who would be first. After that day, the picket line taunted and jeered him, but let him through. Working Dog worked hard and long hours to keep the store running, and a month later, when the striking employees returned to work, they found that Working Dog was their boss.

26. BO / Separating
(*Bullshit/Apprehension*)

Be wary of joining

You must recognize and remove yourself from stagnant associations in order to build more useful ones. Seek more personal relationships rather than connections through groups; the latter do not foster growth, they squelch it. When you join a group in hopes of personal advancement, at best you will expend a lot of energy for a minimal gain. When you join a cause for a supposed greater good, you accept the stigma of that group's voice and actions, and represent ideals that perhaps do not mesh entirely with your own. If you see yourself foremost as a member of a certain profession, cause, ethnicity or any other broad category, the sense of belonging that you gain is at the expense of your growth as an individual.

The band provided Working Dog and other members with an enjoyable escape from their day jobs. From the beginning, all had agreed that any money made from playing locally would be saved to pay for a group trip to the islands for a beach bar band tour.

As plans came together for the trip, The Bass Player was hesitant. "I can't afford to go," he said.

"We'll chip in so you can," the others said, but The Bass Player made other excuses. It soon became clear that he just wanted his share of the money, even if it meant that the band would not stay together for the trip, or for that matter, stay together at all. They divided the money, and the band fell idle.

A month later, Working Dog received a call from a booking agent, who said that a well-known group was coming to town for the music festival, and that the agent was recommending that Working Dog's band open the show.

Working Dog brought the remaining band members together, and proposed that they regroup for one last performance, and include The Bass Player.

"He destroyed the group," one said. "We need to get a different bass player."

"Whoever we would get wouldn't know our songs," said Working Dog. "We wouldn't be as good as we could be, and we can't give the headliners and audience anything less than that. This is an opportunity we've all dreamed of, and if we're going to do it, we all need to put our resentment aside and bring The Bass Player back in."

It was difficult, but they shelved their emotions, and the event was a memorable success and the perfect swan song for the group.

27. SONG / Conflict
(Bullshit / Anger)

Eliminate emotion as a thought process

Differentiate between passion and emotion. Good emotions such as enthusiasm, love, and joy fit under the umbrella of passion. This is all positive energy that you should nurture and share.

On the negative energy side, you have emotions such as anger, jealousy and fear that, unchecked, will drain you and those around you. If you're upset about something, the first thing you must do is take the emotion out of it. If you don't, you'll say something stupid. Retreat to collect your thoughts and separate the emotional components; you will see that they are relatively small and manageable. Find a rational resolution. Never deal out of negative emotion.

As he sat on the beach, Working Dog saw a young swimmer being swept out by an undertow. Although The Swimmer desperately fought the rip, his efforts were futile.

Working Dog ran to the surf and swam to the young man, who in a panic still tried to fight his way back toward the beach. Working Dog locked one arm around The Swimmer, and swam parallel to the shore until the two were out of the undertow's force.

"There's no way you can fight a riptide directly," explained Working Dog once they were on shore. "You have to overcome your impulse, keep your head, and move across it, not against it, until you are out of its force."

2⅞. ⅱGEN / Stillness
(Bullshit/Distraction)

Avoid emotion sickness

You are an emotional being. Not only do you deal with your own emotions, you tend to accept other people's emotions. Don't. Passion is the only emotion you should pass onto others. Likewise, it is the only emotion you should absorb.

Let people come to you for decisions, direction and support, but do not let them make you a sponge for their negative emotions. When they transfer their emotions, negative people suck the energy out of those around them. They can ruin spirit, productivity and even entire companies. Let these people vent steam, but don't pick up their banners without truly understanding what is behind their problem. Probe them logically, and you will often find that the real issues are different from what they first seem to be, probably an accumulation of things over time.

Positive energy grows exponentially. Share it, and ally yourself with people who have it. Keep your distance from those who do not.

Working Dog was frustrated by the incessant complaining of several employees whose antics were beginning to affect the attitudes of other workers. He brought all of the employees into the conference room.

"I'm going to quit," Working Dog told them.

"Why?" they asked in shock.

"Because you're a bunch of whiny piss-ants. Everybody's complaining about each other behind their backs. Those of you who are listening to others whining are just as guilty, because you're letting it fester," explained Working Dog, who then adjourned to his office.

Over the next two days, the employees came one-by-one to Working Dog's office. The ones who did nothing wrong accepted blame and apologized for it. The main culprits denied it and blamed others. The whining stopped for a while, and when it resumed, no one listened.

29. MING YI / Blocking the light
(*Bullshit/Confusion*)

There is no middle in which to be caught

You tend to feel that you are caught in the middle. If you accept this, you have only yourself to blame.

You constantly deal with multiple forces, balancing, uniting or bypassing them on the way to a result. You are caught in the middle only if you don't have an opinion of your own, and you accept the opinions and emotions of others. Offices and families are Petri dishes for this. If you're going to listen passively to someone talk about someone else, you ARE getting caught in the middle. If people have problems with someone else, tell them to address those issues with those people directly. You will always have whiners, but as long as you don't get involved, and you inspire others to ignore those people, balance can be maintained.

"You ever notice how every family has one kid who's a screw-up?"
philosophized The Drummer. "In my family, it's me. My brother runs a
tech company, my sister's a lawyer. They both make a bundle.
The only thing my parents got me to make is trouble."

"It's not the circumstances that shape you, it's how you react to them," replied
Working Dog. "Two soldiers can share a POW cell. One could end up a
mess for the rest of his life, the other could be a senator. Two people can
be exposed to the same germs, and only one will get sick. If your attitude
is weak, you have a better chance of being infected by adverse
circumstances. It's not the stimulus, it is how you react to it, and
whether or not you allow it to fester."

"What are you saying, I'm not a failure, I'm not a success, it's all
my fault or it's not my fault?" mused The Drummer.

"You're probably the best drummer I've ever played with," said
Working Dog. "In that respect you are a success. But the fact that you
see yourself as a failure for not being like the rest of your family
IS your own damn fault."

3☉. JIE / Deliverance
(Bullshit/Ego)

Don't add fault to the wounds

Okay, your parents screwed up. Now get over it.

As long as you blame someone else for your shortcomings, you have not accepted responsibility for your own life.

Most children are born good. Most parents try to launch healthy, well-balanced, responsible, productive young adults into the world. As they reach adulthood, most offspring could argue that their parents' effort wasn't good enough. Whether this is true or not, at this point it is irrelevant. As soon as you are on your own, that story is finished. There are no more excuses. Keep the good, disentangle yourself from the bad, and start over. Get on with your life. You can change anything. You cannot be someone else's fault any more. Once you accept that, you have control.

Working Dog and several competitors vied for the contract to construct The Owner's large office building. One presented a colorful schedule that straddled an entire wall of The Owner's office.

"Look at what your competition gave me," said The Owner to Working Dog. "What are you going to do for me?"

Turning his attention to the byzantine schedule on the wall, Working Dog asked, "Can you read that? I can't, and I've been in this business a long time. If you can understand it, give them the job. If you can't, you have two good reasons to hire me. First, I won't bullshit you, and you'll know exactly what's going on at all times. Second I'll make the same deal with you that I make with all of my customers: if I don't do what I say I'm going to do, you can kick my ass, because that's what I'm going to do to my people if they don't do it."

31. XIAN / Influence
(*Interaction/Distraction*)

Use direct lines

The path to success is surprisingly direct. Find out what your market needs, determine how you will deliver it, promise those results to the customer, deliver on your promise, and have fun doing it. This is the way to earn and sustain good business. If your heart and mind are in the right place, and you are open, direct and fearless, good fortune will come to you.

Also available is business that is not as good. This is work awarded to people willing to play whichever game the customer fancies, often in the form of a superficial parade of suits and flamboyant presentations disguising little substance. Pomp and fluff are favored by customers who find comfort in familiarity rather than thinking for themselves. If that is what impresses that prospect, find another one, because someone more pompous and fluffy than you is bound to come along.

"Did you get hold of The Painter?" Working Dog asked.

"I emailed him a couple times but he still hasn't responded," said The Project Manager.

Working Dog called The Painter's cell phone twice before it was answered. "Sorry to interrupt, but we need to move your schedule up a day and have you on site tomorrow," said Working Dog. "Can you do it?"

"I don't know, that might work," said The Painter hesitantly.

"That's great," said Working Dog. "I really need you out there. So we'll see you there tomorrow morning?"

"Yeah, I guess," said The Painter, evidently busy and anxious to attend to other matters at hand.

"I really appreciate it," said Working Dog. "I'll see you tomorrow morning at seven o'clock, right?"

"You got it," said The Painter. "Tomorrow morning, seven."

"Thanks for understanding," said Working Dog.

32. LÎ / Clinging to the Fire
(*Bullshit/Frustration*)

Use light to see more clearly, but don't get drawn into the fire

You are giving technology too much control over you. The advantages of communication technology are to access, impart or manage information more efficiently. But as you become more reliant on less personal media, you can distance yourself from important relationships.

Recognize the difference between applications that accelerate and those that add layers or distance. When you have the option, use the phone rather than emailing or texting. Unless you wish to document a point, you will achieve more by speaking directly with someone. Emails are often ignored. When they are read, people tend to infer meanings you may not have intended, so you must choose your words carefully.

You may have to tell someone something three times to ensure that it gets done. You might accomplish that in three emails, or you can be assured by one conversation.

V. HANDLING MORONS

We love those elephants and we love those mules
We let those politicians make all the rules
We follow blindly, and we pick a side
And that's where all the bad men hide.

Divide and conquer, keep them apart.
Keep them angry, keep them at war.
Keep them separate and they'll never know
What it is they are fighting for.

> *Lyrics from **Move to the Middle**,*
> *By James Gentile*

Although he was a couple years out of school and had only a two-year degree, Working Dog was managing the plant's tool-making, troubleshooting machinery, and routinely doing other tasks beyond his daily responsibilities as a product designer. He asked The Department Head for an assistant, but instead they hired him a new boss who had an advanced engineering degree from a prestigious college. Working Dog's workload continued to grow. Again he went to The Department Head to ask for help.

"Your boss seems to have extra time," said The Department Head, "why don't you give him some of your work?"

Working Dog gave The Boss an easy project: design a jig that would hold two small plastic cylinders to be joined by an air compressor.

Although it should have taken less than a day to design and fabricate the tool, it was three weeks later that The Boss unveiled an oversized mold made of hardened tool steel that cost several thousand dollars.

"What are you doing?" asked Working Dog. "All we needed were two small pieces of aluminum that you could have pulled from the scrap bin. Why did you use tool steel?"

"It's a tool, isn't it?" said The Boss.

$33.$ ZHÊN / Unsettling thunder, but no rain
(*Morons/Distraction*)

Weary of irrelativity

There is a difference between wisdom and knowledge. Practical knowledge and common sense are not measured by degrees. Aptitude, attitude and appetite are more meaningful than educational credentials. People who have learned to think for themselves are more useful than ones who can only spout theories.

Most experienced engineers cannot do the first calculus problem they got in college, because they never used that knowledge again. They never used it because it was irrelevant, as were the next five calculus courses they had to take. Discipline after discipline, generation after generation, students are taught how theories are derived rather than applied.

Education is most useful when it relates to practical application. Unless you dream of inventing new theories, this type of coursework is practically worthless. Teachers have an ideal opportunity to show students why they should care, to teach students how knowledge can be functionally applied, how to get things done and get others to get things done. They are in a position to teach young people how to get along with others from all walks of life. In this respect, most educators fail.

The company was preparing to introduce a new connector that
Working Dog had developed while working as a product designer.
The complex tooling that The Boss had procured from an outside
source had some problems, but Working Dog modified it so it
would work. Once the parts were in production, there were
problems with assembly. The Boss studied the problem and tried
several adjustments, but they were unsuccessful, and his bosses were
becoming anxious. Working Dog went to the people on the
assembly line, who explained that separate minor problems
with tolerances, sequencing and assembly speed were the issues,
and that the modifications made so far were not addressing
those points. To them the problems were obvious, but no one
else had asked them. Working Dog went to
The Boss with the solution.

The millionth connector was soon produced, the stock
surged, and, just as Working Dog expected,
the company threw a big party to honor The Boss.

34. GÛ / Repair what has been decayed
(*Morons/Frustration*)

Avoid corporate inertia

Most large corporations that excel do so by functioning as an affiliation of small businesses that run almost autonomously, manageable groups where people hold themselves and their coworkers accountable. Others are dinosaurs being kept alive by the stock market. When corporate leaders worry more about investors' perception of their stock than real profits and losses, their companies run like glaciers, slowed by politics and posturing.

In a big company, it is important to align yourself with the right people. These aren't necessarily the ones who wield the most power or influence. They are the people with positive energy. Good people want to be accountable. Bad people don't. Keep your distance from the ubiquitous politics, ass-kissers, cynics and other black holes that dominate corporate space. They can draw you in and wear you down.

When you design new products, it is usually wise to use as many existing parts and tools as possible in order to minimize new engineering. This was the case with a gauge that Working Dog was assigned to develop. He went into the plant and found a watch-sized movement gauge he wanted to study. As he walked back toward his lab, someone abruptly shut down all of the plant machinery.

"He's carrying a part!" shouted two union workers.

The pair blocked his way until The Plant Manager arrived and admonished, "Parts must be carried by union workers."

"Then here is your fucking part," said Working Dog, handing it to one of the union workers. "I quit."

As Working Dog started to clean out his desk, his supervisor apologized for the misunderstanding, and asked Working Dog what it would take for him to stay. Later that day, he got apologies from the union workers and The Plant Manager. Out of respect for the customer, Working Dog went back to work on his gauge, and on the day it was completed, he quit.

𝟥𝟻. GE / Revolution
(*Morons/Anger*)

Quitting time

Unless all you seek is a paycheck, stay with a job only as long as you are learning, growing, and moving toward becoming the person you want to be. If you cannot run your department as a business and make your people accountable, move on. If your boss routinely stifles your ideas or takes credit for them, move on. If you cannot isolate yourself from the politics, move on.

With a new job you will find a new system. There will be good things about it. Embrace what works. There also will be bad things about it. Once you understand the system, use your new perspective, creativity and personality to try to change it positively. If those above you are smart and secure, they will welcome your ideas. If they are not and they block your way, move on, because otherwise you will spend the rest of your career at a dead end where you will stop striving, learning and caring.

Unions were hitting one of Working Dog's construction jobs, picketing and harassing other workers and destroying equipment. One evening, as 32 union representatives sat in a council meeting, Working Dog walked into the room.

"I've worked with many of you," he began, "And I want the rest of you to see the face of the guy you're fucking with." He went on to explain how he hires reliable people who will do what they promise, be they union or non-union.

The Carpenters' Agent noted that twenty years ago, the first job he visited was Working Dog's. "He invited me to sit down and have a cup of coffee," explained the Business Agent. He said, 'I don't have any work for you now, but I'll always be honest with you, never lie to you.' He eventually called me with work, and he has always been honest with me."

Many others around the table agreed with The Carpenters' Agent, but one still complained, asking, "Hell, what do I have to do to get a job from you, get you a hooker?"

Working Dog asked, "Would that be a high class union hooker, or one of those non-union shanks?"

36. JIAN / Impasse
(Morons/Apprehension)

On account of ability vs. unaccountability

"How many people work here?"

"About half."

Even in the most ponderous of bureaucracies, you will find capable people who are not brought down by the inertia of those around them and the system within which they work. Seek out these people, value their efforts, and treat them with respect.

Unions could be great things. They all could be groups of the most skilled and dedicated people in the profession, so good that no one would want to hire anyone else. Instead, many have become shelters where success is often measured by how little one must work in order to receive a paycheck.

When people stress that they are union, you have a problem. If they stress that they are non-union, you have a problem as well. They both miss the point: What you want to hear is what they are going to do for you, and why they can do it better than anyone else. What you seek is the demonstration of competence and the confidence that they will keep their promise.

Despite an exceptionally long wait getting approvals, the large project was completed on time, and the state's business development office proudly publicized the complex as a model of international cooperation. They asked Working Dog what they could do for him in the future.

"The hardest thing about any construction project is always getting permits from the state," said Working Dog. "If you could make that faster and less of a pain in the ass, you'd have a model that would actually help build something."

37. LV / Searcher for Individual Truth
(*Morons/Confusion*)

Don't buy the party pack

Put your trust in individuals, not groups. For a nation founded on the principle of being run by the people, the U.S. government has remarkably few individuals. Instead, it is overwhelmed by two posturing armies of blowhards that have divided and conquered the nation. Most elected representatives are not there to represent their constituents; they are there to sustain the existence of their party, whose platform is leased by various other interests.

Do not buy into a party package. Stand by your beliefs. Take the time to find and ally yourself with the few individuals who have the courage to think for themselves and who share your ideals.

"Sorry I didn't get back to you," said The Supplier after Working Dog called him, "but I'm wearing a couple extra hats today. You know how it is. There's only so much you can do, even for a world-class multi-tasker."

"That reminds me," said Working Dog, "of a few other clichés that never made any sense to me.

"The first is, 'opposites attract.' Whether I'm looking at a supplier, employee or customer, I favor people whose ethics and attitudes complement or match my own, rather than oppose them. In business, the only things that opposites attract are aggravation and trouble.

"'Work on your weaknesses' is another one. In business, this can be a recipe for mediocrity. The key to success is to focus on your strengths, and not try to be 'all things to all people.'

"And then, 'There's only so much you can do.' This is an excuse, and in business, 'there are no excuses.' If you promise something, 'do whatever it takes' to deliver it.

"To make a long story short: If you are going to give me clichés instead of the answers I need, you are not like me, and not likely to attract any more of my business."

38. GOU / Coming to meet
(Morons/Resignation)

Don't be seduced by clichés

The world is pocked by large groups of people who gather like fungi, united by the same buzz phrases and getting nothing done.

Clichés don't work. They may seem harmless, except that people who heavily favor the phrase du jour tend to substitute that for actually thinking and working. They presume that their audience will infer credibility and deeper implications from a phrase that so many others embrace. In practice, clichés don't do the job, and neither do the people who substitute them for answers and actions.

"Don't count on us being there tomorrow," said The Excavator. "The weatherman's calling for rain. I'd like to reschedule for Friday."

"It might rain," said Working Dog. "It might not. Here's what you do. Tomorrow morning you walk outside and look up at the sky. If your face is wet, it's raining. If it's not, get your ass to the job site."

39. FÛ / Turn back
(*Morons/Overload*)

Turn off, tune in

The media is the mess, and values drawn from it have little true currency. Commercials relentlessly create new ways to suggest that a product will get you laid or paid more than you're getting now, and create standards for constant gratification and adulation that are unattainable. If you count on the news for your perspective of the world, you can't avoid the disquieting sense that hoards of murderers and lunatics are framing earth's destruction. Even the daily weather is routinely hyped up to the status of a major event.

Everyone who communicates on a mass scale has an agenda. Not all have nefarious intentions, and not all are even aware of it, but everybody spins. By only seeing things in others' lights, you resign yourself to darkness. Look past the pixels to see the light. Trust what you see, not what it shown to you, and your vision will be clearer.

"I don't know what it is, but God must have had a good reason to keep me from getting the promotion," sighed The Relative.

Working Dog raised one of his arms and spun it around his head several times.

"Why did you do that?" asked The Relative.

"I don't know," said Working Dog. "I guess that since God is up there controlling everything that everyone does, he just wanted me to lift my hand over my head and wave it around."

"That's ridiculous," said The Relative.

"Hey, I think you're onto something," said Working Dog.

40. T'AI / Peace
(*Crossroads/Apprehension*)

Holy crap

Each of us needs an outside light to help the inner self maintain balance and courage, to remind us that we are not on the top of the heap, that we are just part of the whole universe. Many people find this peace, harmony and strength in religion. However, problems arise when people equate this to giving up control, and think that The Higher Force is routinely tinkering with their lives, on hand to interrupt the physics of the universe to guide a field goal, pick lottery numbers and boost careers. When fueled by fear, guilt and self-doubt, religion can breed stagnation and become an excuse for lack of responsibility, with fate to blame for failure.

VI: WINNING OTHERS OVER

You're hired for work, you're hired for pay.
Don't keep no promises. It's okay.
You're stealing money from the man.
He's got so much, and that's why you can.

Justify, everybody do it. Justify, it's the way of the world.
Justify, everybody do it. No need to worry, just justify.

If you like this song and think it's true,
You're the one I'm talking to.
I'll kick your ass and make you cry.
And then I'll just turn and justify.

> *Lyrics from Justify,*
> *By James Gentile*

Early in his career, Working Dog worked for a construction company that treated its customers royally, but its employees poorly. The managers' lack of respect for the workers created an adversarial environment, and the employees had no incentive to take pride in their work or their company. Because the turnover of good people was high, the quality of the work suffered, and the company eventually lost their treasured reputation among their customers.

The next company for which Working Dog worked treated its employees very well, but constantly beat up its suppliers on price, and avoided paying them as long as possible. They soon found it difficult to get materials on time. Schedules and budgets were seldom met, and they eventually lost their reputation among customers as well as suppliers.

When he started his own company, Working Dog vowed that he would treat all three side of the business fairly and with respect. Over the years, his profits were never the windfalls that his predecessors had sought, but his business and reputation grew steadily.

41. BÎ / Unity
(Pressure/Greed)

Think in the Triangle

The personal side of business is actually three sides: the customers, the employees and the suppliers. Many companies feel that, in order to be more profitable, one of these sides must get screwed. This is wrong. The quick gain in profits is eventually offset by the loss of quality, commitment and reputation on the affected side.

Success is more gratifying and longer sustained when all three sides are treated fairly. Build partnerships with people you trust and respect, and who will treat you the same way. When everyone shares that attitude, and the passion of the leader holds the sides together, you have the strongest possible model for success. When issues arise, you need to be able to always look at all sides, keep an open dialogue, and find the best solution. A little pressure just makes the triangle stronger.

When The Hotel Developer told Working Dog that they had selected another
contractor with more experience, Working Dog surprised the prospect by
offering his services to watch over the other contractor.

"Why would you want to do that?" The Hotel Developer asked.

"Number one, I like you guys and if I can't do all of your work, I want to at least do
some of it," said Working Dog. "Number two, I guarantee that I'll save you more than
my fee. Number three, I figure that sooner or later the guys you chose will screw up,
I'll come in and save your ass, and you'll give me every other project you do."

Working Dog was hired to oversee the project. Several months later the group
was meeting at a critical point, when the other contractor admitted that the
revised schedule still wasn't done.

"It takes a lot of time to do it right," said the other contractor, eliciting
groans from the others.

"Let's do it now," offered Working Dog. He turned over a page from the report
and outlined the flow of the trades, starting with two weeks for the carpenters
to frame the top floor, followed by the plumbers and electricians, drywallers
and onward as the coordinated work flow cascaded down to the lobby.

For twenty minutes he asked questions as he worked, then passed the hand-drawn
chart to The Hotel Developer. "I'll have a nice, computer-generated version
for you tomorrow, but here's your schedule," said Working Dog.

In the years that followed, Working Dog constructed many hotels for them.

42. XUN / The gentle, constant wind
(Crossroads/Frustration)

Add corners

Don't try to make more money by cutting corners. When you are frustrated with a job, don't ask yourself, "Is this acceptable? Will the customer buy it?" Rather than cutting quality, ask yourself, "What can I do to add value for the customer?"

In the long run, you will succeed by adding corners. This does not refer to changes in plans or specifications, but to the little extras that you contribute to a project. Little things that go beyond the original scope of work but help out the customer don't have to cost much money to pay a good return.

When the job is done, the customer remembers two things: 1) Did you do what you said you were going to do?; and 2) was the process enjoyable?. When the answer to both is "yes," that is what they will relate proudly to their friends and associates. That is what will make every customer a referral for new business.

Early in his business, Working Dog had misread one of his customers. As a job was nearly done, The Customer insisted that they renegotiate everything. So much money was owed to subcontractors that Working Dog had no leverage.

"Don't take it personally," said The Customer. "This is business, and I'm teaching you a valuable lesson."

Although he lost money, Working Dog finished the project as he had promised. Several years later, The Customer called him again. "You are the best builder I've ever worked with, and I'd like you to give me a price on a new project."

Several days later Working Dog called The Customer with a price. "It's twice what I normally charge, and I'll need half of the money upfront," explained Working Dog.

"This is outrageous," said The Customer.

"This is business," said Working Dog. "Don't take it personally."

43. YÍ / Source of Nourishment
(*Need to Lead/Greed*)

Price yourself consistently

Look for opportunity, but do not be tempted or distracted by opportunism. Price your services the same way every time. If you overprice your work when demand is high, people will not come to you when the economy is slow. Without a trusting customer base, you then will be forced to price your work below market value, and your resentment will compromise the quality of your work.

Successful businesses are built on relationships. Assume that every customer is going to come back, and most will.

Working Dog was invited to a wine tasting party in New York. As The Host talked about each wine being served, most of the guests effusively repeated and rephrased his words.

As the evening drew to a close, The Host said, "I have a special treat, one of the most expensive bottles of wine in the world."

A small glass was poured for each of the guests, who were in turn asked for their comments. In colorful terms, they praised its rich bouquet, rewarding mouth and splendid finish.

"This tastes awful," opined Working Dog as the other guests shied away.

The Host paused a moment, then smiled and said, "He is correct. The rest of you are trying too hard. This WAS a great bottle of wine, but it has turned. The most important point I can leave with you is not to be swayed by others' opinions. If you like it, it's good wine."

44. ZHONG FU / Inner Truth
(*Interaction/Resignation*)

Open for improvements

What you like about other people can tell you about yourself. Perhaps you admire the way someone interacts with others, the way some people can do math in their heads, the way somebody doesn't talk very much. Take what you like in others and try to work those things into your own personal structure. Some won't fit, but others will connect.

While ignorant people are inclined to kill things they don't understand, wise people will constantly seek to expand their knowledge. Yet there is balance that must be maintained. Always try to understand, but don't try too hard, and do not be apologetic for your likes and dislikes. Observe others, but think for yourself, and have the confidence to make your own evaluations. You can learn much from others without parroting their opinions.

"I'm building another bowling center in your area, and you've been highly recommended," said The Prospect on the phone. *"Have you done this sort of project before?"*

"I have not," said Working Dog.

"That's too bad," said the Prospect. "I was looking for somebody who has the experience and knows the industry."

"I can appreciate your concern, but you'll find that I learn fast, and I think it would be worthwhile for us to meet anyway," persisted Working Dog. Although he was hesitant, The Prospect eventually agreed to meet the next day.

As soon as he hung up the phone, Working Dog drove to The Prospect's other bowling alley. He found The Maintenance Man, explained the situation, and asked if the man would show him around and tell him how the place worked. The Maintenance Man felt honored by the attention and respect, and proudly explained the nuances of operating a bowling alley as he took Working Dog through the center. When they finished, he lent Working Dog several reference books to study that night.

The next day, Working Dog spoke authoritatively about the concourse and settee, and matters critical to a bowling center's operation.

"I thought you never built a bowling center. How do you know all this?" The Prospect asked.

"Your maintenance guy told me," said Working Dog. "Just because I didn't know yesterday doesn't mean I don't know today."

45. QIAN / Modesty
(Interaction/Apprehension)

Tap the power of "I don't know"

When a question is asked, most people venture an answer, even if it is a guess. There is nothing wrong with saying, "I don't know." The important thing is what you say right after that.

"I don't know, but I'll find out," can be a very intelligent response. The humble phrase is so seldom heard that it commands attention. It is an opportunity to demonstrate honesty and responsiveness as you learn something new.

Working Dog was still numb from the previous night's bout
with dehydration, the result of a long day in the Caribbean sun,
capped with a midnight hike up the mountain to toast
the full moon. He was uncharacteristically quiet
as he and The Guest walked around town.

In the spice shop, they saw a sign. It said:

Be profound, funny, or quiet.

"Most people find that advice incomprehensible," observed
The Guest. "If people stopped criticizing and correcting
everyone else, the world would be mighty quiet."

"When someone corrects me, I tell them 'it's my fantasy, stay
the hell out of it.'" laughed Working Dog. He realized
he had been quiet too long, and his humor began to return.

46. XIÂO GUO / Small Things
(*Interaction/Frustration*)

Correct selectively

Your words carry value. Spend them wisely.

Words come in various denominations. Jokes are small change, fun to spend and a modest investment in a pleasant experience. On the other extreme, critical words can be very costly, and don't go away after they are used. As in a chess match, critical things you say can affect you many moves later.

Control your impulse to criticize and correct others. Whether or not you agree with someone or some action, as long as it is hurting no one, let it go.

While on vacation in Maine, Working Dog and his wife were hiking with their young children when they came to a trail that went up the mountain. They felt that they had adequate food and time, and their two daughters were eager to tackle the challenge. But the climb was arduous for the children, who had to rest often until Working Dog carried the younger daughter the rest of the way to the peak. The parents then realized that the only way they would be able to descend before nightfall would be to take a more direct route down.

When they found a steep but manageable gravel slope, Working Dog and his wife each clutched one of the children to their chest, and made a series of controlled slides down the mountainside. By the time they reached the base, the parents' jeans and shoes were shredded, but the children arrived safe, unscratched, and jubilant.

"I can't believe I climbed the whole mountain!" the younger daughter cheered.

"I'm impressed," smiled the aching Working Dog. "You showed that you can do anything you put your mind to."

Many years later, the younger daughter had risen above a long and difficult personal crisis. Working Dog and his wife expressed their pride in her.

"It was tough," said The Daughter. "There were times that I didn't think I'd make it. But then I'd say to myself, 'I climbed Mount Katahdin. I can do anything.'"

47. DING / The Cauldron
(*Interaction/Overload*)

Share your credit line

If you take all of the credit for the effort of your team, the next time that they must follow, it will be at more of a distance.

Greater things can be accomplished when you don't care who gets the credit. Share it liberally with those on your team, and you will nurture confidence and success, which are self-perpetuating. Each goal that a person achieves becomes a steppingstone for the next one.

In response to The Customer's request that the project be accelerated, Working Dog used extra strong, high early concrete so the steel could be set sooner. The following week, Working Dog got a panicked call from The Customer.

"An associate informs me you can't set steel on concrete for at least four weeks," said The Customer. "We're on our way to your office with The Township Inspector."

The three men marched brusquely into Working Dog's office, where The Associate shared his knowledge of concrete.

"I can understand how you feel that way, but you don't have all of the facts. We used special concrete that gets to the proper strength in four days," said Working Dog as he laid out the specifications and test results for inspection.

The Township Inspector took several minutes to review the data. "This is absolutely fine, excellent work," he said.

Working Dog thanked all three of the men. "You're welcome to ask me questions or bring people out any time you'd like," he added.

Later that day, he received a call from The Customer, who apologized. "I also want to thank you for not giving it back to me and my friend. You had every right to, but we were embarrassed enough already."

"No problem," said Working Dog. "It was an honest mistake."

"I guess you're right," laughed The Customer. "As I recall, when I first gave you the job, I told you I was going to be the biggest pain in the ass you ever worked with. At least I was right about that."

48. K'UI / Opposition
(*Interaction/Anger*)

Respect your adversaries

You will find adversaries in life, even though you do not seek them. Treat them with respect, and you will greatly enhance your ability to work around them. It is seldom wise to attack, even if you have the upper hand and an aggressive personality. When a confrontation arises, do not act out of emotion. Step back until you can look at the situation objectively. Seek a solution that can achieve your goals while allowing your adversary to make concessions with a level of dignity.

VII. LEADING WISELY

A friend of mine's a seeker, a seeker of the light.
But as he got enlightened, he noticed quite a site:
The people all around him, they couldn't find their way,
And it just drove him crazy, crazy every day.

Be careful what you ask for, it might be what you get.
Watch out what you're wishing, it might hurt a bit.
Be careful what you're thinking, slow down your thoughts.
You're thinking you're escaping, but you just might get caught.

*Lyrics from **It Might Be What You Get**,*
By James Gentile

The ideal location for the proposed medical center was a 28-acre tract near the hospital, but it was said to be impossible to develop. Many others had tried and failed.

Working Dog and his team laid out exactly what would have to happen, in what order. He first went to a homeowner who successfully fought the last effort at development. After hours of friendly conversation with the man and his wife, Working Dog described his plan for the tract, how the traffic would not compromise the family's privacy, and how the project would likely increase the value of their property. He asked about any other concerns they had, and showed how the project could be modified to accommodate them. The couple felt like they were part of the plan, and agreed to support it.

The property straddled two municipalities that for years had bickered over its water, sewage, traffic, stormwater, and tax matters. Working Dog showed them how these issues could be resolved to the benefit of both. The municipalities felt like they were part of the plan, and agreed to support it.

In the same manner, Working Dog personally worked with the department of transportation, turnpike commission, DEP, Army Corps of Engineers, retail stores and other parties, addressing each one's concerns, making them feel part of the project, and earning their support.

The deal was done and construction began with much media fanfare. All of the parties involved were invited to the groundbreaking ceremony. One at a time, each approached Working Dog and said the same thing to him: No one thought this property could ever be developed, and it was hard to believe that he had made it possible.

Working Dog had the same response for each: "I just brought people together. YOU were the one who made it possible."

49. DA CH'U / Great Involvement
(*Leadership/Ego*)

Lead quietly

One does not have to go very high in business to be ineffective as a micromanager. If you try to drag people by the nose, they will resist you. If you rely on pressure and intimidation to make others do what you wish, they will lose incentive. Force cannot achieve positive change nearly as effectively as people can change if they wish to.

Even if you own the whole company, look at yourself as a leader, but not as the sole owner. Every business is comprised of employees, suppliers and customers. The best leaders do not force their way with any of these partners, including the employees. Good leaders inspire the others, present them with goals, set up ways for them to find pride and purpose in the effort, and guide them to making the right decisions.

Try to manage without reminding others that they are being led. After success is achieved, when they look back and see how you brought it all together, they will respect you all the more.

"When do I get my written evaluation?" asked The New Employee after two months.

"Haven't I been evaluating you every day?" asked Working Dog. "If you want a written evaluation in this company, just take notes."

໒໐. HUAN / Gentle dispersion
(*Leadership / Distraction*)

Evaluate your people every day.

If you review each employee's performance yearly or quarterly, you leave a long period for problems to incubate and fester. Employees tend to be defensive, and criticisms taken personally. You also establish a system similar to television sweeps months, when networks strut their best performances for a short period, and deliver mediocre fare the rest of the time.

Evaluate your people every day. Never micromanage, but constantly stay in tune with how they are handling their workloads and where they may need help. Daily face-to-face meetings gently minimize obstacles and misunderstandings, and remind each employee, including yourself, what is expected.

The Canadian Company had decided to work with another contractor for their new plant. Eight months later, Working Dog received a call from The Broker who had orchestrated the initial meetings, and who had steered The Canadian Company to the other firm.

"The customer is in trouble," said The Broker. "They've had meeting after meeting, but the contractor still doesn't have a handle on what the customer wants, and they're returning to Canada in two days."

Working Dog brought The Canadian Company to his office the next afternoon. He asked them many questions about what they wanted and needed, and where the project was stalling. He took careful notes, and told them to come in the next morning before their flight.

Working Dog and his team stayed up all night. At nine the next morning, they presented a printed proposal and drawings, summarizing what The Canadian Company said they were seeking, and showing how it would be possible to achieve those goals.

"That's exactly what I want," said the leader of The Canadian Company. "We went through eight months of meetings with the other contractor. How did you get it all in one day?"

"We listened," said Working Dog.

51. JI JI / Caution after crossing the stream
(Leadership /Overload)

Don't overmeet

In order to maintain your balance and productivity, avoid situations and inferior influences that can derail or distract you, such as unnecessary meetings. If the head of the meeting is focused, disciplined and unhesitant to stop digressions, a large meeting can still be brisk and worthwhile. If not, the volume of attendees will exponentially affect the speed with which the objective is met, if it is met at all.

Every meeting should have a stated objective. If the organizer cannot define the objective beforehand, or if the objective sounds nebulous or contrived, find a way to get out of the meeting because, in the currency of useful information or contribution, you will be fortunate to get even a small return on the time you invest.

Working Dog asked The Applicant which two people in the world he admired most, and why. After he responded, The Applicant asked the same question of Working Dog. Although he had asked that question to others dozens of times, Working Dog had never before asked it of himself.

"I admire Pat Croce," said Working Dog after a moment. "He was a trainer for the Philadelphia Flyers and Sixers. Then he got a job with a local radio station, and parlayed a fitness show into a network of health clubs. He's an inspiring speaker, always positive, always upbeat. He goes and goes; he doesn't believe in giving up. When I was young, one of my goals in life was to buy the Sixers. Pat Croce did that. He talked with the owner for years, saying he wanted to buy the team, and the owner kept saying no. Then one day, the owner didn't say no. He didn't say yes immediately, but the moment he didn't say no, Pat Croce knew the team would be his.

"The other person I most admire is my wife's stepfather. He's always happy, always smiling. He is constantly appreciative of all the little things around him. He sees the good in sunshine, the good in rain. Most people always want more, and ignore the beauty around them. He wants nothing more than what he has around him at that moment.

"They seem opposite, but perhaps I admire these two people because they have the qualities that I always strive to improve and balance within myself. Good question, by the way."

52. WU WANG / The Unexpected
(*Leadership /Confusion*)

Hire aspirations

As you interview prospective employees, rather than talking about your company and looking for their reaction, get your applicant talking about other things. Ask unexpected questions. People come to interviews prepared to tell you how great they are. Once that is out of the way, have them tell you what they are not good at. People who are not honest with themselves will say, 'I can't think of anything.' Assure them that there are a couple hundred things that you do poorly; surely they can think of a few. People who know themselves may describe their strengths and weaknesses as the same thing without even knowing it.

Hire the person whose personality best fits your culture, who has positive energy, and who will do whatever it takes to get things done. Look carefully for the ability to learn, since you will have to retrain them to your own methods and style. Above all, trust your gut.

Working Dog had hired an old friend who was down on his luck and needed a job. As site supervisor, The Friend worked out well for nearly a year, but he eventually destabilized. Despite several conversations and warnings, he repeatedly screwed up. Working Dog knew he had to fire The Friend.

"This is one of my best friends, and I'm going to end up in a fistfight with him," worried Working Dog as he walked toward the field office where his friend waited. He opened the door, and said nothing for a moment.

"It's about time you showed up," said The Friend. "I'd have fired my ass a long time ago."

53. DA ZHUANG / Great power
(*Leadership / Resignation*)

Protect your TIRFF

The first time you need to fire someone, you won't sleep well for several days before and after. If it is a fundamentally good person that you are letting go, it may seem inhuman to hurt that person for the mere efficiency of a system you call your business.

But the longer you carry that person, the more obvious it will be that your inaction is even less fair to many others. Other employees work hard, yet see the same rewards going to those who are not as capable or committed. Your customers pay you for your services, the quality of which will eventually suffer. It is unfair to all of these people to carry anyone who delivers anything less than the best.

The essence of the manager/employee relationship is Protect Your TIRFF: Teach. Inspire. Require. Flourish or Fire. You must be willing to teach and inspire; employees need to flourish and rise to the required level. If they cannot, let them go. If you do not, you and all but one will eventually be the worse for it.

The Developer introduced himself on the phone and described his project. "I want estimates from five builders, and you were one of the ones recommended. I'd like to send over the specs and get a price from you."

"When I work with a customer, we practically live together for a year. Don't you want to meet me first to see if we connect?" asked Working Dog.

"I'm very busy," said The Developer. "I checked out the firms that I am calling, and you all have good reputations."

"So you are going to hire someone for a project that will cost you millions of dollars, based solely on a price?" recapped Working Dog.

"Like I said, all five of you have good reputations, and any one of you will be fine," said The Developer.

"That's good," said Working Dog. "Since you'll be just as happy with any of the other four, I won't bother."

5*4*. JIE / Limitations
(*Leadership / Frustration*)

"Just the price" is wrong

Personal commitment is important to keeping every relationship, in business as well as your personal life. In the former, the price is just a part of what you offer. Passion, service and trust are equally important assets that add value to the relationship. Remain aware of all of the different facets that create your value, and grow by building relationships with others who recognize them. Do not waste your efforts on those who "just want a price."

People who buy solely on price believe that everyone is the same. Those who don't value others usually don't value commitments either. Price honestly, emphasize that it is only one component of your value, and avoid people who don't recognize it.

They were ready to start the six million dollar distribution center when The German Company that had contracted Working Dog advised him that they were divesting the other local operation that they had originally offered as the lease guarantee. Working Dog asked the customer to designate another operation as security for the bank, but The German Company did not respond.

Several days later Working Dog was visited by a high state official, who had been contacted directly by The German Company. "This project is important to the region. It'll bring 400 new jobs, and be a model for other European companies to follow," said The Senior Policy Advisor. "It's a big, well-known company, and The Governor and I feel we should proceed without the collateral."

By "we," The Senior Policy Advisor meant "you."

Working Dog got The Banker on the speakerphone, and explained the visitor's recommendation. "I don't know about you," said Working Dog, " but I don't feel like having my policy advised."

"I don't want my policy advised either," agreed The Banker.

Working Dog hung up, and said to the Senior Policy Advisor, "If 'we' are that sure, I'm sure the state will have no problem guaranteeing the loan."

This evidently made the state less sure, and the next day the Governor's office regretfully informed The German Company that the project would cease until the lease was guaranteed. The company expressed dismay, but shortly thereafter offered another operation as collateral.

䷄. XV / Waiting for Nourishment
(*Morons/Ego*)

Be allergic to carrots

Some customers will say, "Let's save the budget on this job so..." and go on to propose that you lose money on a project so you can make much more money on a much bigger project later. You will never get that carrot. Don't bite.

Similarly, others may cite a spirit of cooperation to intimidate or coerce you into making poor decisions. People who truly value others' services will not force seriously compromising propositions. Don't be bluffed. In the face of such challenges, either hold your ground or walk away.

The Department Heads noted that every time they met with one particular assistant, she left with little to do, while the Department Heads had even more to do. Since The Assistant often had little work, and the company did not have strict office hours, she routinely left for the day before many of the others. When Working Dog realized who was managing whom, he fired The Assistant.

Several weeks later, The Office Manager came excitedly into Working Dog's office. "I found a great policy handbook," she said. "It details rules for every imaginable situation so problems like we had with The Assistant don't happen again."

"We fixed that situation as it needed to be fixed, and that's the way we'll do it if it happens again," said Working Dog. "We will always have only three rules here: Do your best, have fun, and don't bitch."

56. MÊNG / Folly of Youth
(*Leadership / Apprehension*)

Rules are made for the bad people

Good workers have high expectations of themselves. Because they find the notions of poor performance and failure to be repugnant, they need only occasional guidance, not close supervision. Like governments, companies tend to make rules to control the behavior of bad workers who might take advantage of latitude in the system. But the more rules you have, the more you discourage the good people and tempt them to leave. Differentiate between rules and expectations. If you surround yourself with good people you can trust and upon whom you can rely, and you make your expectations clear, you will not need many rules.

VIII. HANDLING SUCCESS

The eagle soars above it all
High above the game
You can have your right and wrong
It still remains the same.

The eagle soars above it all
He sees it all so clear
You can have your back and forth
The eagle's almost near

The eagle soars above it all
He's got it figured out
As you argue on and on
The eagle leaves no doubt

The eagle soars above it all
How about you?
If we could drop our foolish pride
We could too.

*Lyrics from **The Eagle Soars Above It All**,*
By James Gentile

In the early days of his business, Working Dog was sharing his woes with two of his friends.

"My customer is holding me hostage," rued Working Dog. "He talked me into building this huge mansion for him as a favor. He had me pay his bills for tax reasons. Now he's not paying me back, and he knows I can't stop because he has me so much in debt. I'm working there day and night."

"We liked you before you started this business, we liked you when you made it a success, and we'll like you if it doesn't work out," said The First Friend.

"I admire you," added The Second Friend.

"How can you possibly admire me in this situation?" asked Working Dog.

"You're life can't possibly get any worse," said The Second Friend. "You've got nowhere to go but up."

57. T'ONG RÊN / Fellowship
(*Success/Overload*)

Everyone needs fluffers

As your success grows, you see changes in others' attitudes toward you. Some change for the better, some for the worse. The best are the attitudes that don't change at all. These reflect the true friends who will provide a touchstone to help you keep your balance. People with whom you have this affinity will help you avoid getting caught up in your success when you are up, and buoy you when you are down.

In the adult film industry, the girls who keep guys up between scenes are called fluffers. When you are feeling down or negative, you need people around you who will help lift your spirits, because no one can always be up.

"The Customer still hasn't chosen which lobby concept he wants to go with," said one of The Partners to Working Dog. "It's holding up the whole job. I think we need to WTF him."

Working Dog called The Customer, and asked, "Yo, what the fuck?"

"What?" replied The Customer.

"What the FUCK?" emphasized Working Dog.

The Customer correctly assumed that Working Dog was referring to the lobby concepts. They discussed the options and picked a style, and the project proceeded back on course.

The following week, on the day they were to go golfing, Working Dog was faced with a work issue that commanded his presence. He called The Customer and left a message apologizing for having to send a replacement for the foursome. An hour later he got a message from The Customer: "Yo. What the fuck?"

升 SHÊNG / Pushing Onward
(*Success/Distraction*)

Stay grounded

For your activity to prosper, your perspective must stay firmly grounded in what is true, real and presently most important. Do not let distractions obscure the vision of your guiding principles. Develop mechanisms with the people with whom you work day after day, triggers that help to bring everyone back to center when they go on tangents and lose perspective of what is important.

"Why did you bring a partner into your business?" asked The Relative. "You built that company yourself, business is booming, you love your work, and you're still pretty young. You ARE the business. Why are you giving part of it away?"

"The employee that I made partner is great at what he does, and deserves to run a company. If it's not this one, he'd probably find another one some day", said Working Dog. "But it is in my own best interest as well. Business owners who structure their companies too tightly around themselves, and boast, 'Without me, this company couldn't survive,' are fools. When they quit or die, they ultimately screw their employees and customers.

"At first I was proud that nothing could happen without me, but now it upsets me. I look forward to the day when there's nothing my company can't accomplish without me. That means I'll have more time to spend with family, play music and travel. When time becomes more valuable than money, you can make your life richer by taking less of the latter."

59. FÊNG / Abundance
(*Success/Apprehension*)

There's no time like the present, no present like time

If you worry more about keeping what you have than about continuing to grow, you are setting up yourself for inevitable disappointment. If something is full, it can't become fuller, only emptier. If you don't continue too expand or refill the container, it's only a matter of time until its contents start to evaporate.

Enjoy the moment, but don't become preoccupied about preserving it. If your life is so abundant that you want and wish for no more, enjoy it to its fullest, but recognize that it must ebb, and don't despair. It's just another law of nature. Embrace the future rather than yearn for the past, and you will find the opportunity to redefine success and achieve great happiness again.

Working Dog liked that most of the island residents tended to take each other at face value, with little concern given to wealth or position. It was in this atmosphere that Working Dog had become friends with The Guitarist, and would often play with his group on Friday nights. But after several months, Working Dog noticed a change in The Guitarist's attitude.

The cause of the tension became evident when Working Dog was praising a new restaurant, and The Guitarist replied, "I wouldn't know, I don't have your kind of money. I saw your house a couple weeks ago, up there on the mountain, overlooking the bay. Man, it's beautiful, but that's a different world than I live in."

Although there remained some distance in the relationship, they continued to play together. One day Working Dog invited the group to practice at his house. As the evening wound down and they finished practicing their song list, the musicians took turns soloing tunes of their choice. Working Dog played and sang about a father who had worked for the railroad for forty-two years.

"That's a great song," said The Guitarist. "Who wrote it?"

"I did," said Working Dog. "It's about my dad."

"I didn't know that," said The Guitarist. "I thought you were a trusty. So you didn't grow up rich?"

"The opposite," said Working Dog. "I never thought of myself as poor. We just didn't have a lot of money. Anything I have now I earned from my construction business that I started in my twenties."

From that point on, they resumed a friendship based on face value.

60. DA YOU / Possession in Great Measure
(*Success/Greed*)

When you got it, share it, stow it or stuff it

Wealth alone can be a burden when it comes to earning true respect. Conspicuous wealth may suggest that you did something that made others want to give you a lot of money, but this is frequently not the reality, and many people today realize that. Still, when you project wealth, many people will treat you differently. Some will be resentful; do not confuse this with hatred. Others will be deferential in the hope that some money will rub off on them; do not confuse this with respect.

True respect is earned by actions and character. If you've earned your wealth through vision, cleverness or hard work, worthy people will respect your actions. If you treat others generously, while being modest about your own prosperity, worthy people will respect your character. If you try to earn respect by merely flaunting wealth, you will attract the interest only of those just as shallow.

The township had the reputation as being the most difficult in the valley for new construction. While many developers fought with the commissioners and complained about the grueling process, Working Dog routinely sent drawings beforehand and did whatever else he could to make their jobs easier.

One day Working Dog called to discuss a new project, and The Township Supervisor offered to meet with him that afternoon. Instead of going to the conference room, they met in the official's office. But it was a friendly meeting as usual, and when they disagreed on points, they discussed them with humor.

As the meeting came to a close, The Township Supervisor said, "I know we can be a pain in the ass. I appreciate you keeping your sense of humor about it."

"You guys aren't a pain. You just want everything done by the book. Anybody who complains about having problems with you guys just hasn't read your book."

As Working Dog was leaving, The Township Supervisor said, "Just keep laughing. It makes our day."

61. ZE / Two Lakes
(*Success/Frustration*)

He whose laugh lasts laughs last

Most of your decisions and actions are made to enhance, directly or indirectly, the feelings of joy or pleasure. There is a difference. Joy comes from the inside, from senses of achievement and self-worth. You want as much of this as possible. Pleasure comes from external forces, from other people and objects that emotionally, intellectually or physically nurture your contentment. In the search of pleasure, you will find many temptations that promise momentary gratification but do not instill joy. Recognize the difference.

Laugh often. It adds an element of pleasure to every endeavor, increases your support and resolve, and helps you to overcome challenges and difficulties. Therein lies joy.

For many years, Working Dog had used music to balance the pressures of his job. He wrote songs and played with friends. They formed a band, and all enjoyed the camaraderie and escape that the practices offered. Although music was still only a hobby, they recorded a CD, and they were getting more and more gigs. But with the money came squabbles, and eventually the group disbanded.

Without his escape, Working Dog devoted more time to his business. He began avoiding social engagements, preferring to work. Although business was booming, he became bitter and critical, and his sarcasm turned to cynicism.

One day he ran into one of the other band members. As they talked, they realized that they were both bogged down in the same negative emotions. The importance of the balance that their music had kept in their lives was suddenly obvious to both.

The next week, Working Dog called The Friend. "I've decided I'm going to do my own CD. If you're interested, I'd love to have you join me."

"That would be outstanding," said The Friend. "When can we start practice?"

62. BÎ / Grace
(Success/Confusion)

Balancing acts

Every movement must be counterbalanced, and the stronger each action is, the stronger the counterbalance must be to keep your footing. Accept who you are, but never stop striving to improve. Be constantly aware of everything around you, but do not be distracted from your course. Don't micromanage, but don't lose touch with your people. Work toward your long-term goal, but focus on one task at a time. See the big picture, but never lose sight of the little details. Be passionate about your work, but enjoy the people in your life.

Your work can be a huge part of your life, but an hour talking with a friend can balance ten hours of stressful work. Ultimately, it is the balance of drive and contentment that determines success.

Despite Working Dog's offer to source and coordinate all of the tradesmen,
The Customer insisted on selecting the architect and subcontractors.
The project progressed erratically, slowed by frequent squabbles between
the various parties. One day Working Dog entered the construction trailer
to find one such argument brewing between The Customer, architect, and
three subcontractors, all of whom were blaming each other for the problems.

Working Dog listened for a moment, and then boomed, "Everybody shut up!
I don't give a shit who did this or who didn't do that. I don't want to hear
anyone else whining about it, either. Here's what we're going to do."

He detailed for each person in the field office what had to be done.
When he got to The Customer, Working Dog said.
"All you have to do is let me handle it."

The Customer looked at Working Dog and said simply, "Outside."

As the two men left the construction trailer, Working Dog
braced himself for an ass chewing.

"I've been meaning to tell you this for a long time," said The Customer.
"You're like an eagle. You fly above all the bullshit, you keep moving,
you don't care about who's right or wrong. You just get the job
done, and that's what I hired you for. It's not my nature
to be hands-off, but I'll try to stay out of your hair."

63. GUAN / Contemplation
(*Success/Ego*)

Soar above it all

Success is determined not by how many responsibilities you handle, but how you handle them. When goals aren't achieved, overloaded slates or outside forces are usually blamed. Incorrectly so. More often than not, the culprit is ego, and the jealousies and insecurities that can go along with it.

Everyone wants to be right. That's human nature. But when a problem or disagreement degenerates into an argument over who is right or wrong, you aren't getting closer to the solution. You're getting stuck. Rather than getting bogged down in an interminable battle of egos, the key is to fly above that morass until you have an objective view of the critical issue. Focus on it, swoop down on it, move egos aside and straighten out the problem, and get back on your way.

1. Inner Peace. When riding a motorcycle, it is important to be in the moment, keep the mind free and clear of life's problems, and be totally engulfed in the ride.

In life we must do the same. We are much more effective when we keep our minds clean of our perceived problems, and focus on the here and now. 99% of our potential problems never happen except in our own minds.

2. Balance. In both life and motorcycle riding, everything has its place. As events turn, it is our sense of balance that lets us know what is here, what is coming, and how to be in harmony with it.

3. Slow Down to Speed Up. To navigate the curves, you slow down as you approach the bend, then accelerate through it. In life, we must handle our problems as curves. Slow down to analyze the problem, figure out your angle, then accelerate through the solution, one curve at a time.

4. Goals. When riding long distances, intermediate waypoints help to keep you motivated on your way to the final destination. In life, short-term goals help us appreciate each stage of life, while our long-term goals give focus to the experience.

5. Attitude is everything.

In summary, find your inner peace, keep your balance, slow down to speed up, and ride "with bugs on your teeth," grinning as you enjoy the full experience of life.

64. JIN / Progress
(*Success/Resignation*)

Ride with bugs on your teeth

Life's similarities with riding a motorcycle begin with the components of the word:

MOTOR: The body apparatus or brain functions that direct purposeful activities.
CYCLE: A period of time that completes a repeatable process of growth.

Likewise, you can define life as, "the brain function that directs the purposeful activities and the process of growth." Our minds can limit or nurture our growth as individuals. Our minds can create stress and obstacles, or overcome them.

The parallel builds momentum when you consider the five qualities needed to fully appreciate the art of riding a motorcycle.

Jim Gentile has been a fan of Eastern philosophy in general, and the *I Ching* in particular, since he was twenty. He credits much of his personal growth and business accomplishments to its teachings. *The Bit Ching Book of Change* offers the reader insights into how he did it, and how others might be able to apply the same principles to their own lives.

Jim Gentile and Russ Slocum have been friends and business associates since the early 1990s.

James Gentile is founder and president of North Star Construction Management Inc., (www.northstarcm.com) and the affiliated development company Polaris Properties, Inc., both located in Allentown, PA. As of this writing, he also owns all or part of several medical centers, a couple industrial parks, an assisted living community, record company and various other commercial properties in Pennsylvania's Lehigh Valley. Jim holds design patents for electrical components that he invented. He writes and performs his own music, and plays a dozen different instruments.

Jim and his wife Denise live in Pennsylvania's Lehigh Valley.

Russell Slocum has spent most of his career in marketing and advertising. His first job after graduating from Lycoming College, Williamsport, PA, was with Prentice-Hall, Englewood Cliffs, NJ, where he wrote and designed book jackets and catalogs. Russ spent most of the next decade as a copywriter with ad agencies, with a couple breaks to work as a freelance writer, and publishing articles in The New York Times Magazine, Playboy and Atlantic, among other magazines. In 1983 he started his own ad agency, and in 1986 co-founded Slocum Blatt Advertising, Fleetwood, PA. He established The Slocum Group (www.theslocumgroup.com) in 2004.

Russ and his wife Ann live in Wyomissing, PA.

How to Consult

The
BIT CHING
Book of Change

In the left column, choose the outer force that most closely describes the challenge at hand. Then, in the top row, find the word that best describes your unsettled feeling (inner force). The number at the intersection indicates the chapter to seek for counsel.

Or just pick up the book and read it.

OUTER FORCE ▼ (The challenge you face)	OVERLOAD	APPREHENSION	FRUSTRATION	ANGER/GREED	CONFUSION	DISTRACTION	EGO	RESIGNATION
OBSTACLE	1	2	3	13	6	4	7	8
CROSSROADS	11	40	42	16	12	10	15	14
PRESSURE	19	21	18	41	22	20	23	17
BULLSHIT	5	26	32	27	29	28	30	25
MORONS	39	36	34	35	37	33	55	38
INTERACTION	47	45	46	48	9	31	24	44
NEED TO LEAD	51	56	54	43	52	50	49	53
SUCCESS	57	59	61	60	62	58	63	64

▼ INNER FORCE (What you feel about the challenge)

15080969R10091

Made in the USA
Lexington, KY
07 May 2012